W9-AFX-856

IMAGES
of America

WINTER COMES TO
NORFOLK

For Charlie –
   To my friend who loves
history. Enjoy!
      Love,
      Lauren

            Christmas '97

On February 9, 1947, fields and low-lying areas were enveloped in a layer of soft snow, which had blanketed the earth quietly and steadily overnight.

> "Snow falling and night falling fast, oh, fast
> In a field I looked into going past,
> And the ground almost covered smooth in snow,
> But a few weeds and stubble showing last."

—From *Desert Places*, 1936
Robert Frost, American poet (1874–1963)

IMAGES
of America

WINTER COMES TO NORFOLK

Amy Waters Yarsinske

ARCADIA

First published 1997
Copyright © Amy Waters Yarsinske, 1997

ISBN 0-7524-0928-X

Published by Arcadia Publishing,
an imprint of the Chalford Publishing Corporation,
One Washington Center, Dover, New Hampshire 03820.
Printed in Great Britain

Library of Congress Cataloging-in-Publication Data applied for

Neighborhood kids piled up giant snowballs to make a snowman, January 16, 1939.

Contents

Acknowledgments

I would like to extend my profound appreciation to Peggy Haile of the Sargeant Memorial Room, Kirn Library. She facilitated the search for photographs and historical records and made the project one of the most enjoyable I have ever done. Though most of the photographs found in the book originated with the Sargeant Memorial Room, there are a number of privately donated pictures and artifacts and author's personal archives which were used to compile the book. I can never thank my husband, Raymond, nor my children, Ashley Nicole, Allyson Emily, and Raymond III, enough for their indulgence while working on another book. I realized that my own family does realize that authoring books is a profession. My oldest, Ashley, looked at me while I was piecing this one together and said to her father, "Mommy has like a real job, doesn't she, Daddy?" to which my husband quickly replied, "Yes, honey, she really does." Delighted, Ashley went off to bed, and I stayed up until two o'clock in the morning.

Introduction

The decision to look at Norfolk and vicinity from the cold-weather perspective was an easy one. There is nothing more enchanting than old Norfolk under a blanket of snow, and nothing more interesting than our transition from fall to winter, nor more delightful than the coming of spring. In our collective memory is the man standing up to his knees in snow; children having snowball fights or frolicking on the ice in their shiny new pairs of skates; our soldiers and sailors filling the city's streets with their presence and our hearts with their sacrifice; those historic moments in our personal and public history which make Norfolk great; and, the beauty of this city's children and the hope that springs eternal from their faces of so long ago. This volume covers the time frame of 1880 through 1965. In the stifling heat of July and August, we always seem to miss the winter; until it arrives, and then we wonder if spring will ever come. Fall is heralded by the trickling of leaves falling softly to the ground and the crisp chill in the air telling us winter is just around the corner. Winter belongs to the "Snow King," icicles, and snow angels. Santa Claus visits in December, and the holidays take on new meaning when we extend the hand of fellowship to another human being. Children are the happy harbingers of spring, with flowers, milder temperatures, and soft winds bringing back memories of kite flying, Easter baskets, and Sunday church services, or trying those new roller skates and scooters Santa brought Christmas Eve to all the good boys and girls.

Charles Simpson "Charlie" Borjes (1891–1959) captured Norfolk at its best because he saw through his camera lens the best in the people who lived here. He had what historian George Holbert Tucker called, "an unerringly sensitive photographic sense," which captured the nuances of our collective character from the joy in the faces of children, despair during the Great Depression, intrepidity in the face of war, the fear of a foreign enemy, and undaunted patriotism to the challenges of changing economies of scale and political climate. Borjes was the grand master of Virginia press photographers during his tenure with the *Virginian-Pilot* newspaper from 1913 to 1956. Using a Graphic camera stuffed in an old canvas bag, Borjes emphasized technique, not technology. He used to say that new photographers at the *Pilot* might have a chance of working out if they "could only abandon all these modern gadgets and get back to grassroots photographic principles." With his camera, Borjes captured the magic of Norfolk, its spirit and good humor, and the innumerable faces, famous or not, which have molded and shaped the city now relegated to history books and people's memory. The clarity, fine detail, and action captured in Borjes's photography were his trademarks. Unless otherwise noted, the photographs in this volume were taken by Charlie Borjes.

The image of the fire at the ferry terminal on December 26, 1935, brought to mind one of my favorite Charlie Borjes stories (of which there are many), told by Warner Twyford, a contemporary of Borjes at the newspaper. Charlie was covering a fire aboard a ship at the Water Street dock in his early days of taking pictures for the Norfolk newspaper. Borjes climbed to the roof of an adjacent warehouse, set up his camera and, once again, proceeded to fill his flash pan with a powder charge which subsequently set off a sound as mighty as Fourth of July fireworks. A cry went up from firemen below, "My God, it's spread to the warehouse!" The same firemen immediately turned their hose on the warehouse roof and began to sweep it from end to end with a constant stream of water. Borjes started running toward the far end, but the stream was gaining on him. Suddenly, he hit a soft spot in the roof and plunged through, saving him from the water, but not a near fall to his death. To pull himself from the jaws of death, Charlie Borjes spread his elbows and hung on. "Scared me to death and skinned my shins," he would later say, "but the stream of water passed over just then and missed me."

Borjes was a man whose personal foibles ranged from never eating away from home because he liked his mother's cooking to holding off the news desk at least a half-hour, recounting the impossibility of getting the shot they wanted due to poor lighting or some other phenomenon of nature. Despite all his foibles, grousing, and adventures—or maybe because of them—he never returned from his assignments without the perfect picture. Charlie Borjes has given immortality to the people, buildings, and even animals that were part of his world and of Norfolk's past. He photographed what we want to see and much of which we would like to remember.

Amy Waters Yarsinske

This "ghost image" was created by the deterioration of a 5-by-7-inch glass plate negative. The scene was shot at the corner of City Hall Avenue and Granby Street, February 27, 1924. Shulman's, located on the first floor of the Monticello Hotel, is on the left.

One

Fall Leaves,
Winter Is upon Us

"The green elm with the one great bough of gold
Lets leaves into the grass slip, one by one . . ."

—From *October*, 1917
Edward Thomas, English poet (1878–1917)

Members of the Tidewater Pleasure Club were photographed during an oyster roast at Cape Henry *c.* 1896. While some enjoyed raw oysters on the shell, others indulged in Lynnhaven oyster stew and, of course, beer. (Photographer unknown.)

There was nothing better to eat in days gone by than a Lynnhaven oyster. Cape Henry was the capital of oyster eating because of O'Keefe's Casino. O'Keefe's was on the oceanfront side-by-side with Chesapeake Transit Company's train station. The watermen tonging for oysters in this photograph were probably on the east side of the Lynnhaven River when the picture was taken in the fall of 1909. (Photographer unknown.)

LYNNHAVEN OYSTER STEW
1 pint (16 ounces) of Lynnhaven oysters, undrained
1 quart milk
3/4 teaspoon salt
1/2 teaspoon pepper
1/2 cup butter
Paprika
Drain the oysters, reserving the liquid in a 2-quart saucepan. Bring the liquid to a boil. Add oysters, milk, salt, pepper, and butter. Salt can be added to taste. Cook, stirring constantly, until butter melts and oyster edges appear to curl. To serve, spoon into bowls; sprinkle with paprika, if desired. Yield: 8 cups.

Children pause from playing by the fence around Beechwood Place, a small park between Pembroke Avenue and Warren Crescent, located at the southern end of Colonial Avenue in Ghent. The photograph was taken in 1895 during Ghent's development. The large house on the right was the home of W.H. Doyle, cashier of the Citizens National Bank. Fergus Reid, a cotton merchant, owned the house in the center. Beechwood Place took its name from the beech trees which grew in profuse numbers on Commodore DeBree's estate, Lilliput, which once stood on the site occupied by the Reid home. DeBree was a Confederate navy officer. (Photographer unknown.)

The cornerstone of Christ Church was laid on October 28, 1909, with religious ceremonies led by the Right Reverend Alfred M. Randolph, Bishop of the Diocese of Southern Virginia, with secular rights conducted by Norfolk Masonic Lodge No. 1. The first service in the new Christ Church took place on Christmas Day, 1910. This was the third church building occupied by this Episcopalian congregation. The first Christ Church was built in 1800 on Church Street, now known as St. Paul's Boulevard, across the street from the 1739 Borough Church. When the church burned to the ground in 1827, a new church was erected at the corner of Freemason and Cumberland Streets, and it was the building from which the congregation moved when the third Christ Church, located at the corner of Olney Road and Stockley Gardens, was completed in 1910. The designation of Christ and St. Luke's Church came in 1935, when the congregation of St. Luke's Episcopal Church, located in Ghent, joined with Christ Church. (P.M. Taylor, photographer.)

President William Howard Taft visited Norfolk on November 19, 1909. He was here to attend the Second Annual Convention of the Atlantic Deeper Waterways Commission. The city fathers had public buildings dressed out in bunting and flags to greet him. The old Norfolk City Hall and Court House, completed in 1850, was perhaps one of the most beautiful of the buildings dressed for the occasion (shown here). Taft and the presidential party wound up their meeting with a lavish party and reception at O'Keefe's Casino on the Virginia Beach oceanfront. Taft rode by train and upon his arrival at the little train station, was taken the 100 yards of brick sidewalk between the station and O'Keefe's by automobile to the restaurant. The car, owned by Charles J. Colonna, had been transported by flatbed rail car to the station prior to the president's visit. (Harry C. Mann, photographer.)

President Taft and his party arrived in Norfolk and were taken to the starting point of a parade in the president's honor, located at the corner of Brooke Avenue and Granby Street, November 19, 1909. (Harry C. Mann, photographer.)

The presidential parade proceeded through Norfolk and had progressed to the corner of Main and Granby Streets when this photograph was taken. (Photographer unknown.)

Good friends posed for this picture behind houses at the 500 block of Mowbray Arch in 1910. From left to right, the boys are as follows: (front row) Henry Lewis and Mac Jenkins; (back row) Jimmy Jordan, Bolling Stanley, and Peyton May. (Photographer unknown.)

The Norfolk College for Young Ladies on the corner of Granby Street and College Place was chartered February 20, 1880, and opened that year with 125 students. John L. Roper was the first president of the board. After the college closed in 1899, the building became the Algonquin Hotel and, later, the Lee Hotel. The photograph was taken about 1910. (Harry C. Mann, photographer.)

Harry C. Mann photographed the famous arched lights on Granby Street about 1910. The arch lighting system was installed in 1910 and used until 1925 from Charlotte to Granby Streets and from Main to Church Streets. As Norfolk obtained larger firefighting equipment, particularly ladder trucks, the lights limited their access to potential fires and had to be removed. Renowned Italian opera star Enrico Caruso came to the city in 1920 for a performance, and he stayed at the Monticello Hotel (visible on the right side of the picture). As he left the hotel for his evening performance and looked upon the lights on Granby Street, he nodded his approval and remarked that the city fathers were kind to light the streets in his honor. The people of Norfolk were so pleased to have Caruso performing in the city that no one attempted to correct his assumption.

Hopkins Fish & Oyster Company, founded by William H. Hopkins in 1895, was engaged in the production, packing, and shipping of fish and oysters. Hopkins had started out in the oyster packing business in 1891 with Alfred A. Jordan at Ludlow's Wharf. The firm was called Hopkins & Jordan. Four years later, Hopkins formed his own company and in 1907 was joined by his son, William Jr. Located in Norfolk's Atlantic City, the company's original oyster house on Water Street gave way to a packing plant, wholesale house, and lime furnace. By 1922, Hopkins Fish & Oyster Company had a three-story brick house at 426 York Street on a lot that extended into the Hague, where Hopkins maintained his fish boats. A retail store was opened on Monticello Avenue in 1918. The Great Depression ended the Hopkins' packing and wholesale business, and by the late 1930s, the retail shop was all that was left. The retail store closed its doors on June 3, 1964. R.L. Hopkins, William's other son, invented the Hopkins Lure in 1948, a fishing lure prized by surf fishermen and sold throughout the United States. (Photographer unknown.)

In the shucking department of Hopkins Fish & Oyster Company (shown here, *c.* 1912), the oysters were opened, graded into classes according to size, and placed in strainers. Fresh water was run over the oysters and a paddle used to swish them about to remove foreign matter. Cans of oysters were packed in crushed ice in barrels and boxes shipped to all parts of the United States and Canada. (Photographer unknown.)

An unknown photographer took this picture of workers trying to stay warm at the corner of Water Street and Commercial Place, December 1913. Though not unseasonably cold, outside laborers felt the chill of downtown winter winds and biting December temperatures. Norfolk was preparing for Christmas when this picture was taken. Most of the shops' decorations had not as yet blossomed into the full range of vibrant colors which usually appeared on city streets for the Christmas season.

New York Governor Alfred E. "Al" Smith responded to the crowd at Broad Street Station on his arrival in Richmond, Virginia, by waving his famous brown derby from the automobile in which he and his wife and Governor Harry E. Byrd of Virginia moved through jammed streets in the capitol. The *Virginian-Pilot* dispatched photographer Charles S. Borjes to Richmond on October 11, 1928, to photograph "the first Democratic presidential nominee to invade the 'solid South' in 80 years." Herbert Hoover, Smith's Republican opponent, won the election.

Burrow, Martin & Company Rexall Drug Store owners and employees were photographed in front of their store at 330 Granby Street, November 1932. Burrow, Martin & Company was established by John W. Burrow in 1850. He opened his first drugstore on Church Street, the primary retail street in the city at that time. Burrow died in 1896, and W.R. Martin purchased half interest in the business and a partnership was formed with John W. Burrow Jr., son of the firm's founder. This partnership continued until 1905, when the business was incorporated with W.R. Martin as president; John D. Burrow, vice-president; W.A. Jones, treasurer; and H.G. Murphy, secretary. When the picture was taken, W.J. Rogers (left, center) had become president, and W.A. Jones (right, center), vice-president.

Kate Smith, famous radio entertainer, sang over the Columbia network from Norfolk station WTAR on Sunday, October 15, 1933, as part of the farewell program for Rear Admiral Richard Evelyn Byrd, renowned explorer, and key members of his party on their Second Antarctic Expedition. The expedition departed from Norfolk for Little America in the Antarctic days later. Kate Smith came to Norfolk in person to present Admiral Byrd's mother a bouquet and to sing "Boy O' Mine," among other songs.

Little Billy Foster found a lost marmoset wandering in front of the Norfolk Division, College of William and Mary, on October 29, 1937. Marmosets are the smallest and prettiest of all South American monkeys. Children love them, as anyone can tell by looking at this young child playing with his new discovery. Found primarily in Brazil, the marmoset is about 8 inches long with a furry body and a foot-long, bushy tail, which is carried like a plume. Marmosets do not use their tails for climbing. They have very human-like little faces and hands and winglike tufted ears. If you came upon one, especially wandering Norfolk, you might think it looked much like a squirrel. This marmoset was quite black in color, though most of them are generally black with gray grizzle produced by white fur interspersed with the black.

Halloween hobgoblins thronged downtown streets the evening of October 31, 1938. Granby Street was the center of the bedlam for young adults and teenagers. Little fellows David Earl Gardner of 1512 Granby Street and Ray W. Gardner of 308 Duncan Avenue enjoyed a stroll, appropriately dressed as an old pirate and jack-o-lantern.

Children at Garrison Williams School dressed up for Halloween, October 31, 1950. Most of the Halloween activity was centered in downtown Norfolk along Granby Street as youngsters and young adults invaded the business district to have a good time before trick-or-treating. One little girl asked a policeman, "If I ring somebody's doorbell and run away, how about that?" The policeman replied, "Just so you don't create a disturbance."

Cheesecake and the Turkey was a photograph staged as one the newspaper's pinup pictures, *c.* 1950. Page-three pinup girls were popular throughout the 1940s and 1950s, and these images reflected an appreciation for the female form.

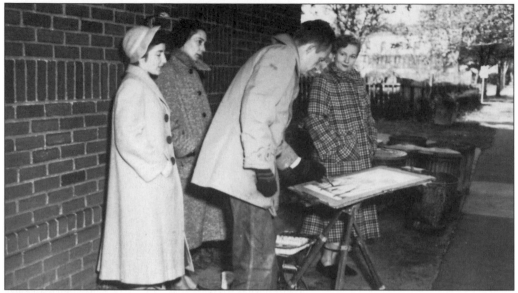

Artist Kenneth Harris (1904–1983) was a familiar site on Norfolk street corners as he captured the lifeblood of the city's character on canvas. Hardly any street, landmark, or vista escaped his artistic eye. He was painting Christ and St. Luke's Episcopal Church at the corner of Olney Road and Stockley Gardens when this photograph was taken on November 21, 1950. He was commissioned by the Norfolk Museum of Arts and Sciences board of trustees that November to paint a series of watercolor pictures of local scenes and activities for the museum's permanent collection titled *Norfolk—1950*. It was not unusual for Harris to be surrounded by passersby as he painted, nor did he mind discussing his projects with his audience.

An East Ocean View family of eight was left homeless and destitute on November 22, 1950, from a fire that gutted their tar-roofed bungalow at the end of Collins Street. Roscoe Williams (a roofing subcontractor), his wife, and six children (ages three to fourteen years) had all their possessions destroyed. The two youngest children, five-year-old Delores Anne and three-year-old Norma Jean, were home when the fire started and had to be rescued by their parents. The Williams family had lived in the house only two months and it was filled with new furniture. The other children in the picture are Christopher Francis, 14; Catherine, 12; Larry, 10; and Jimmy, 8.

King's Turkey Ranch, shown here, was located 1 mile south of Cradock on George Washington Highway. King's advertised young, tender turkeys which had never been on the ground and which were milk-and-grain-fed. The ranch was a popular place to choose a fresh turkey for the holidays. This photograph was taken November 24, 1953.

These eager hounds are ready to hunt, c. 1950. The photograph was taken in conjunction with an organized fox hunt in Pungo.

The Norfolk Fox Hunting Club held frequent meets in and around the city during the nineteenth century. As the city grew and outlying neighborhoods developed, it was no longer possible to hunt on horseback with dogs. The sport continued into the twentieth century, as foxhunting in Princess Anne County and Pungo became increasingly popular and clubs sprung up in beautiful rural reaches of Norfolk. This picturesque scene, *c.* 1950, somewhere in Pungo, symbolizes an era now only part of the past.

Two

Downtown Remembrances

"We many were, but few remain
Of old familiar things,
But seeing them to mind again
The lost and absent brings."

—From *Memory*, 1846
Abraham Lincoln, Sixteenth President of the
United States and poet (1860–1865)

Security Storage and Safe Deposit Company was located at the corner of First and Front Streets. The photograph shown here captured one of the company's familiar horse-drawn wagons on Commercial Place, c. 1910. W.P. Ives and Company, blender of old whiskies, is in the background. (Harry C. Mann, photographer.)

Mary Wilson Chamberlaine married Fergus Reid, a cotton merchant and philanthropist, in 1898. The couple resided at 507 Pembroke Avenue in Norfolk's Ghent section, and from this home, the couple entertained and contributed to the social life of the city. The couple had three children, but one, Janet, died in infancy. Two other children, Fergus Jr. and Helen, prospered in adulthood. Mary Reid is shown here with Helen, c. 1898. (Photographer unknown.)

Helen Reid, daughter of Mary and Fergus Reid, married the Baron Jean de Lustrac of France on November 24, 1925, at which time she became the Baronness de Lustrac. The couple had two religious ceremonies, one Roman Catholic in accordance with Baron de Lustrac's faith and the other an Episcopalian service to satisfy Helen Reid's religious upbringing. Baron de Lustrac was a thirty-one-year-old French army officer. The baronness, twenty-eight years of age at the time of her marriage, lived overseas most of her married life, coming back to Norfolk frequently for visits with her parents. The Baron and Baronness de Lustrac were photographed returning to France after the wedding. (Photographer unknown.)

On November 8, 1914, St. Joseph's Colored Catholic Parish observed the twenty-fifth anniversary of its establishment with a High Mass presided over by the Right Reverend D.J. O'Connell, Bishop of Richmond (front row, center). The Mass was celebrated by the very Reverend Justin McCarthy. Reverend J.H. Dorsey served as deacon, and Reverend Joseph Wareing, sub-deacon and pastor of the parish (front row, left). Father M.J. Ahearn assisted Bishop O'Connell. The priest standing next to the bishop on the right was a United States Army chaplain (Roman Catholic). St. Joseph's parish began in September 1889 on Brewer Street. The first pastor was Father Lawrence O'Connell, uncle of Bishop O'Connell. St. Joseph's parish and school moved from a dilapidated structure on Brewer Street to a new chapel and school on East Queen Street, now known as Brambleton Avenue, in May 1893. (Harry C. Mann, photographer.)

Ladder Truck C belonging to the Norfolk Fire Department was covered and embedded in ice after battling the Monticello Hotel fire, January 1, 1918. The New Year's Day blaze which destroyed four Granby Street buildings, entailing a property loss of more than $ 2 million, killing three firemen, and injuring dozens more, is remembered by most Norfolkians as the "Monticello Hotel fire." The "fire" was actually a series of three fires set in three separate locations. The first building to become engulfed was the Dickson Building at 226–230 Granby Street. The second blaze was discovered in the northwest corner of the Monticello Hotel, followed by another in the Lenox Building and the D. Carpenter Building next door. Down the street in the Granby Theatre, another fire blew out the windows on the lower floor but was quickly controlled. The police department arrested nineteen Germans and turned them over to federal authorities in connection with an arson investigation. German saboteurs were thought to have set all the fires. (Photographer unknown.)

A dinner was held at Norfolk's Monticello Hotel in honor of President-elect Warren G. Harding's victory in the November 4, 1920 Presidential Election. Victory dinners were enjoyable if you happened to be a member of the party that won. Harding, a Republican senator from Ohio, recorded a landslide victory which carried over to the United States House of Representatives and Senate, where Republicans took the majority. The Harding-Coolidge ticket broke the "Solid South" when Oklahoma and Tennessee voted Republican. His Democratic opponent in the election was Governor James Cox of Ohio, and Cox's running-mate was Franklin Delano Roosevelt. Harding had a scandalous reputation as president of the United States, but most of the serious allegations against him did not break until after his death mid-term on August 2, 1923. Calvin Coolidge succeeded him as president. (Photographer unknown.)

The Norva Theatre, located on Granby Street between Market and Freemason Streets, once presented the best of vaudeville and first-run picture shows. The movie playing when this photograph was taken on January 22, 1926, *Tower of Lies*, was a Metro-Goldwyn-Mayer production starring Norma Shearer and Lon Chaney. *Tower of Lies* was released at the end of 1925. In 1979, plans were proposed to convert the empty theatre into a racquetball and health club. The Downtown Athletic Club occupies the building.

The Goodyear blimp NC-7A *Puritan*, part of the company's advertising fleet, flew over the intersection of Granby Street and City Hall Avenue on December 10, 1930. During periods of particularly harsh winter weather which precluded vessels from supplying remotely populated areas such as Virginia's Eastern Shore and barrier islands, these airships were used to ferry supplies and transport sick or injured residents to hospitals on the mainland. When World War II broke out, most of Goodyear's fleet was procured by the United States Navy, including the *Puritan*.

A portion of the army of Civil Works Administration workers mobilized in Norfolk assembled at 16th Street and Monticello Avenue on the morning of Saturday, December 16, 1933, to get their week's pay. There were approximately two thousand in this group, and they received an aggregate payroll of $28,000. By the following Saturday, their number increased by at least another thousand, and the payroll amounted to over $50,000.

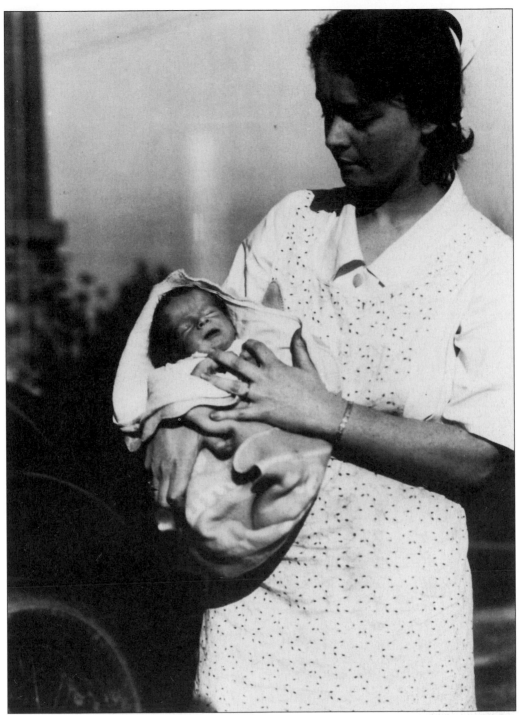

A one-month-old baby, born November 6, 1931, was abandoned in a rooming house at 700 Yarmouth Street on December 7, and placed under the care of the Society for the Prevention of Cruelty to Children when this photograph was taken three days later. Social workers searched for the mother, but were certain she had returned to her home in North Carolina. The baby was thought to be afflicted with polio.

William N. Cox, sports editor of the *Virginian-Pilot*, poses with a chimpanzee friend, December 23, 1933. Cox had just come to the Norfolk newspaper from the Greensboro *Daily News* and, before Greensboro, the *Herald* in Durham.

Georgianna Taliaferro, society columnist for the *Virginian-Pilot*, decided to show-off her version of a cigarette filter and pose for Charles S. Borjes's camera at her newspaper desk, March 31, 1934.

A cake for President Franklin Delano Roosevelt's Birthday Ball was fashioned by D. Pender Grocery Store, where it had been displayed the day before the January 30, 1934 dinner-dance at the Monticello Hotel. Roosevelt was celebrating his fifty-second birthday. A merry lot of some five hundred New Dealers danced and marched then bought raffle tickets for a resplendent birthday cake, the proceeds from the sale of which were added to the admissions as a contribution for the Warm Springs Foundation, an organization which provided assistance to infantile paralysis sufferers. The cake was won by holders of a jointly purchased ticket, William Adler and Bill Lassiter. John Twohy II made the presentation of the cake to the winners. Adler and Lassiter graciously shared their prize cake with partygoers.

The captains of the various school safety patrols shown here joined about seven hundred others at the Newport Theatre on the morning of February 1, 1936, to see safety measures films and *The Silver Bullet*, a thriller showing a 2,000-mile trip of a streamlined train. There were twenty-four schools in Norfolk, South Norfolk, and Norfolk County with safety patrols at that time, each having three officers, a captain, and two lieutenants. Representatives of various civic groups were presented to the children by W.B. Baldwin, chairman of the Tidewater Automobile Association Safety Council. Theatre parties for the safety patrols were held regularly during the school year.

The Works Progress Administration (WPA) was approved by Congress on April 8, 1935, and before its dissolution in 1943, this program would spend upwards of $11 billion, mostly in wages and salaries for nearly 8.5 million people. The WPA, working in concert with other federal agencies, built numerous public buildings, bridges, airports, and parks which remain important parts of communities throughout the United States today. People employed by the WPA were primarily manual laborers, but some of its best known projects were cultural and involved the financing of artists, writers, craftsmen, actors, and musicians. One of the WPA projects in Norfolk, shown here, involved quilt-making and needlecraft. These women were brought to the Boush Street School to do their handicraft. The date was October 15, 1936. (Photographer unknown.)

Dutch carried this little girl happily around Bain Field on a pony ride, November 11, 1938. The occasion was the Bain Field Horse Show, a competitive event and benefit for the Christmas Joy Fund. The show was organized by Hampton Roads horsemen and the Norfolk Legion and Drum Corps. All the well-known show horses in the area were entered in the competition. The show manager was Irving Kline, and the ringmaster, Billy Huxter.

The *Virginian-Pilot* news staff greeted Corporal E. Corbell Jones, former police reporter, on a return visit from Fort Story, where he was transferred to the enlisted United States Army Reserve Corps, December 7, 1941. Jack "Scratch" Brown, newspaper mascot and dog mayor of Norfolk, extended his greetings and best wishes to Jones. Jack "Scratch" Brown's favorite spot for naps and air raid drills at the office was actually under the desk.

Rose La Rose was the premier entertainer at the Gaiety Theatre on the city's East Main Street, Norfolk's most famous—and popular—burlesque house. Photographed in her dressing room, February 14, 1950, the hundredth anniversary of the theatre, Rose La Rose was happy to mug for the camera. Suzette, one of the Gaiety's last burlesque entertainers, once said of Rose La Rose, "Stripping is selling and Rose knew how to sell." The building in which the burlesque performed opened as a theatre known as Mechanics Hall on February 14, 1850. From 1907 to 1936, Mechanics Hall was a vaudeville and burlesque house called the Majestic Theatre, but in 1936, the Majestic began exclusively featuring burlesque acts and changed its name to the Gaiety. Progress brought down the curtain on the Gaiety, January 31, 1961, and so ended over 7,500 nights of suggestively, but tastefully, revealed flesh and ribald humor. The building was torn down a few months later.

Three
In War and Peace

In his 1939 year-end radio broadcast to the people of the British empire, King George VI comforted his people with a quote from Minnie Louise Haskins written in 1908: "I said to the man who stood at the gate of the year: 'Give me a light that I may tread safely into the unknown.' And he replied: 'Go out into the darkness and put your hand into the hand of God. That shall be to you better than light and safer than a known way.'"

Norfolk prepared a grand homecoming for members of the 29th Division and Norfolk Light Artillery Blues who returned from France in the spring of 1919. The city's population poured into the streets waving flags, shouting, singing, cheering, and crying. Downtown streets from Main and Church to Granby and Charlotte were decorated with flags, bunting, and banners. The arch in the photograph was erected over a couple of weeks in April and stood for many weeks at the intersection of Granby Street and City Hall Avenue. (Photographer unknown.)

A streetcar strike by workers of the Norfolk Railway and Light Company in late-February and March 1902 brought out Company D of the 71st Virginia Volunteer Infantry of Hampton, otherwise known as the Peninsula Guards. Members of Company D were part of the First Battalion of the local militia which also included Companies K and L from Portsmouth and C from Newport News. Members of Companies C, D, K, and L were happy to go home. Strikers became violent at times, tossing stones and bricks through streetcar windows. The unit was standing in front of the Park Avenue Presbyterian Church on North Park Avenue near East Queen Street when the photograph was taken prior to their return trip to the Peninsula on March 12. (Photographer unknown.)

The Cadet Corps of Virginia Polytechnic and State University (VPI), nearly five-hundred strong, arrived at Norfolk's Union Station the morning of Saturday, October 7, 1933, to support their football squad in a game against the University of Maryland at Bain Field that afternoon. The corps marched in parade formation down City Hall Avenue, past the City Market and Armory and Monticello Hotel (as shown here), turned down Granby Street and headed to the City Auditorium. VPI cadets had plenty to celebrate by day's end; their football team beat the University of Maryland 14–0.

38

During the First World War, the Norfolk Navy Yard underwent great expansion. Three new drydocks were begun between 1917 and 1919, each of which was completed in 1919. Employment had reached its peak at the yard in February of that year, attaining the record figure of 11,234 for that time, as compared to 2,718 workers in June 1914. To accommodate hundreds of new yard workers and their families, many of whom had relocated from great distances, two war housing projects, Cradock and Truxton, were constructed on the outskirts of Portsmouth. On October 31, 1919, opening ceremonies were held for Drydock Nos. 6 and 7. The photograph shows the admission of first water. (Photographer unknown. Courtesy of Hampton Roads Naval Museum.)

United States Marines were caught relaxing a few hours before boarding the USS *Wright* (AV-1), flagship of the Aircraft Squadrons of the Scouting Fleet, December 7, 1929. The *Wright* transported 490 Marine Corps officers and enlisted men from Hampton Roads for Port-au-Prince, Haiti, to reinforce seven hundred Marines already on duty in that troubled West Indian island republic. The battalion was under the command of Major Louis E. Fagan II and consisted of one hundred twenty-five officers and enlisted men from Parris Island, South Carolina; a detachment of three hundred officers and enlisteds from Quantico, Virginia; and seventy-three officers and enlisteds from the Marine Barracks at the Norfolk Navy Yard. A major portion of the contingent were veterans of the so-called Banana Wars in Nicaragua and Haiti. When asked about leaving so close to Christmas, a Marine sergeant who had served previously in Haiti replied, "Christmas is Christmas, no matter where you spend it."

The first class to go through the Reserve Officers' School at the Naval Operating Base Norfolk, Virginia, were photographed on December 20, 1917. The United States Navy had taken possession of 474 acres of land in Norfolk, including the Jamestown Exposition site, to construct its new naval base and fleet training center on July 4, 1917.

Cyril, a six-month-old chimpanzee, was photographed aboard a United States Navy ship, September 22, 1937.

The Navy-Marine Corps rivalry flared anew with pre-game publicity for a football game at the Naval Base Stadium between the Devil Dogs of the Marine Corps from the Norfolk Navy Yard and the Naval Training Station Boots in a benefit for the Navy Relief Fund. This picture, snapped December 1, 1937, shows "Uncle Billy," a veteran goat and Navy mascot (on the right) with a pair of gobs in tow, and the Marine Corps mascot, a traditional bulldog. Though the scrappy Boots were favored to win the December 4 game, they lost to the Marines, 12–6. "Ten thousand gobs laid down their swabs to lick one sick Marine . . ." so the saying went at the Marines' victory celebration. O.K. Pressley, coach of the Devil Dogs, attributed his team's win to backfield star Jimmy "Dynamite" Falzone of Boston, Massachusetts, who scored both of the Marines' touchdowns.

Wives and sweethearts eagerly awaited the return of their sailors, part of the Battle Force, Atlantic Fleet, which came back to Norfolk after a three-month deployment on April 12, 1939. The expressions of joy on the faces of those in this photograph need no explanation.

Back from three months of arduous war games in the Caribbean, sailors of the Battle Force, Atlantic Fleet, enlivened downtown Norfolk streets. Downtown business streets literally buzzed with activity on April 13, 1939, when this photograph was taken, as thousands of enlisted naval personnel jammed the shopping thoroughfares on their first shore leave stateside in months. New life was injected into the streetlife of Norfolk as gobs, three or four abreast, appeared in an unending parade, hurrying up and down the streets. Some sailors headed for the Navy YMCA on Brooke Avenue, while others spread out to seek diversions of their choice.

Jagged walls and an effluvium of rubble were all that remained of the central wing of the historic Administration Building at the Naval Operating Base on January 26, 1941, after a fire caused by faulty wiring swept the structure. The building was completed in 1907 for the Jamestown Exposition. Rear Admiral Joseph K. Taussig, commandant of the Fifth Naval District, lost his headquarters communication center, post office, district disbursing office, and invaluable records pertaining to critical defense projects.

Fourteen Japanese nationals were arrested in Norfolk on December 7, 1941, almost simultaneously with Japan's declaration of war on the United States and Great Britain. Japanese detainees were kept for investigation and fingerprinting. Military and civilian authorities had compiled a list of Japanese nationals over a period of several weeks prior to Pearl Harbor. Shown in the center of this photograph is Hidemisto Toyota, age fifty-three, a cook in a restaurant at 1103 Church Street owned by Wataru Tada, another detainee. Toyota had been in the United States for thirty-three years and lived in Norfolk for the past ten at the time he was detained. When asked about his reactions to the bombing of Pearl Harbor, he said: "I thought there would be some more of those negotiations."

The first blackout of World War II in Norfolk occurred on December 13, 1941. Civilian Defense authorities announced the blackout without warning to test the responsiveness of merchants and residents of the city. Norfolk citizens cooperated wholeheartedly with the "Black 'em out!" order. The police department's only complaint was that there were too many automobiles on the streets. Operating in heavy Saturday night downtown traffic with dimmed lights and darkened streets led to a few mishaps, none serious.

Children at Robert E. Lee School hurried under their desks during an air raid practice, December 17, 1941.

These enterprising young boys, J.U. Addenbrook's sons, decided to help the war effort by opening their own bomb raid and supply center at the corner of Hampton Boulevard and Westover Avenue, February 3, 1942.

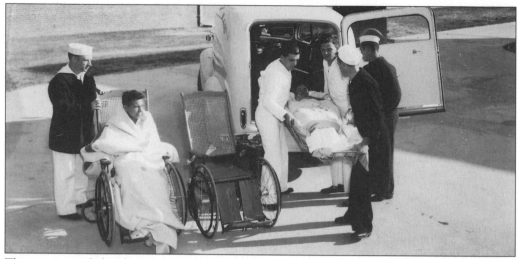

The two wounded sailors in this photograph saw action in the invasion of North Africa and were among the first group of wounded American Navy men to arrive at an East Coast port. Seaman Second Class Oliver Gustafson (left) of Bessemer, Michigan, and Motor Machinist Mate Second Class James Le Grice (right) of Dorchester, Massachusetts, are shown as they left an ambulance upon arrival at Portsmouth Naval Hospital, November 28, 1942. Le Grice, nicknamed "Duck and Dive" by his shipmates, was one of the first Navy commandos to land on North African beaches. He was machine-gunned by a German aircraft strafing the beach from an altitude of no more than 30 feet. Le Grice earned his nickname because he saved his skin so many times ducking on dry land and diving in the water. Gustafson, member of a ramp boat crew which landed troops and jeeps from a transport ship offshore, suffered shrapnel wounds in the leg when a hand grenade he picked up on the beach exploded.

Elias Codd (left) discusses a bond drive with Lieutenant Commander H.L. Harris of the United States Coast Guard, a war bond officer, in his delicatessen at 406 West Princess Anne Road, c. 1942.

Chief Specialist John Philip Sousa II, son of the famous band leader and march composer, led some of his fellow United States Coast Guardsmen in a pick-up jam session, March 19, 1943. Sousa joined the Coast Guard in Norfolk during June 1942, and he served as director of the Post Security Barracks in Portsmouth. Prior to his enlistment, Sousa conducted his own orchestra. Of all the men in his civilian orchestra, Sousa was the only one who did not hold an officer's commission in some branch of the armed forces.

The Smith Street USO was a popular place for African-American service members to unwind during World War II. The facility was completed on March 15, 1942, under the auspices of the United Service Organizations (USO), an organization which supplies social, recreational, welfare, and spiritual facilities to armed service members. The USO was organized in 1941, and its initial existence discontinued in 1947. President Harry S Truman requested the USO resume its services to members of the America's armed forces when the Korean Conflict broke out in 1949. The group was reorganized in 1951 and has been supported by voluntary contributions ever since. This photograph of a jitterbug team was taken sometime between 1942 and 1945 by an unknown photographer.

A captured two-man Japanese submarine was exhibited on Freemason Street between Granby Street and Monticello Avenue on March 25, 1943, in connection with a war bond campaign sponsored by the Retail Merchants Association. At 81 feet long and 17 1/2 tons, the vessel had a cruising range of 130 miles and carried two torpedoes. This particular submarine was captured in the midst of the Japanese attack on Pearl Harbor.

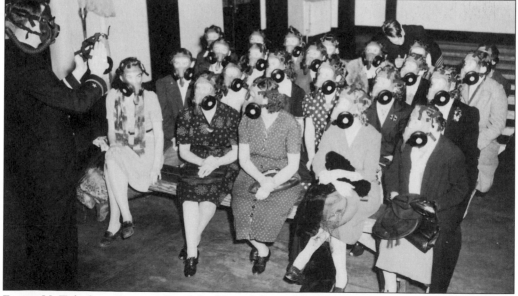

Ensign V. Taliaferro Boatwright of the United States Navy instructs a class of Norfolk women on how to use a gas mask, 1943.

Five flyers from the famous United States Army Air Corps 99th Fighter Squadron were in Norfolk on December 15, 1944, to boost bond sales for the Sixth War Loan in a rally sponsored by the African-American special events committee at Booker T. Washington School. Flyers are, from left to right, as follows: (front row) Captain Maurice Johnson, Captain Charles H. Hall, and Captain Herbert E. Carter; (back row) Lieutenant Willie H. Fuller and Lieutenant Price D. Rice. Hall was the first African American to shoot down a German aircraft and the first to win the Distinguished Flying Cross. Johnson was the squadron's flight surgeon. The 99th trained at Tuskegee, Alabama, and were subsequently called the Tuskegee Airmen. The squadron deployed for the first time in April 1943 to the Mediterranean.

The launching of the USS *Shangri-La* (CV-38) on February 24, 1944, produced one of the largest crowds, estimated at over one hundred thousand people, in the history of wartime launchings at Norfolk Navy Yard. The *Shangri-La* was the first of three aircraft carriers built by the yard during World War II. The keel of the 27,100-ton carrier was laid on January 15, 1943.

In attendance for the launching of the USS *Shangri-La* (left to right) were Colgate Darden, governor of Virginia; Captain J.E. Manch, the only Virginian to participate in the Doolittle Raid on Tokyo; Mrs. Josephine "Jo" Doolittle, the ship's sponsor; and Mary McClellan, flower girl. The aircraft carrier derived its name from the mysterious Shangri-La referenced by President Franklin D. Roosevelt in his radio broadcast after Lieutenant Colonel Jimmy H. Doolittle's famous air raid on Tokyo from the aircraft carrier *Hornet* (CV-8) on April 18, 1942. Roosevelt, knowing the Japanese were listening, suggested the B-25 bombers of the 17th Army Air Force Air Group which hit Tokyo came from the utopia of Shangri-La and not a Navy aircraft carrier 668 miles from the target.

Volunteers staged a Thanksgiving dinner followed by free entertainment for seamen at the USS Fairfax Residential Club at the Fairfax Hotel on City Hall Avenue, November 30, 1944.

Armistice Day, celebrated November 12, 1945, in Norfolk, held special meaning with the end of the war in Europe in May and Japan's formal surrender aboard the USS *Missouri* on September 2. Crowds, seven deep to the curb on either side of Granby Street, watched and cheered as Norfolk's largest assemblage of military units marched past.

Norfolk's Chinese population stole the show at the 1945 Armistice Day parade. An ersatz Japanese Emperor Hirohito, on foot, leading his famous white horse and drawing a brightly decorated cart with Uncle Sam in the driver's seat, was one of the most interesting presentations by any participant in the parade. In front of dignitaries seated in the reviewing stand, Hirohito stopped the horse and bowed, the crowd roaring its praises for Uncle Sam. Though Norfolk's Chinese people planned and staged their entry in the parade, they solicited assistance from large Chinese groups from Washington, D.C., New York, and elsewhere.

PERSONAL CAR

OF

HERMANN GOERING

CAPTURED BY

506ᵗʰ PARACHUTE INF.

101ˢᵗ AIRBORNE DIVISION

SPONSORED BY NORFOLK JUNIOR CHAMBER OF COMMERCE

The supercharged Mercedes Benz belonging to Hermann Goering, chief of Germany's Luftwaffe during World War II, was captured by Lieutenant Jack Holland of Rocky Mount, North Carolina, and his detail from the 506th Parachute Infantry, 101st Airborne Division, three days before Germany capitulated on May 8, 1945, and before Goering himself, then in the village of Berchtesgaden, surrendered. The Mercedes was found in the garage of Goering's hunting lodge outside the town. Holland and Corporal Roderick Smith of Fredericksburg, Virginia, Technical Sergeant Thomas Meggs of Union City, North Carolina, and Staff Sergeant Richard Falbey of Yonkers, New York, members of Holland's detail, took the car on a 5,000-mile tour of the United States that began November 1. As Smith put it, the car was one "sweet-running piece of machinery," with five forward speeds; a top speed of 130-miles per hour; eight-cylinders; dual ignition engine; capable of conversion to diesel; sixteen spark plugs; 230-horsepower; 65-gallon gasoline tank; and twenty-five lights. The Mercedes had 2-inch, bullet-proof glass and thick armor plate beneath and around the occupants, making it weigh over 4 tons. Each door accounted for between 600 to 700 pounds of the load. Thousands of people looked at the car in the Selden Arcade on December 11, 1945. It was brought to Norfolk under the auspices of the Junior Chamber of Commerce to stimulate Victory Bond sales.

The aircraft carrier USS *Midway* (CVB-41) arrived at Naval Station Norfolk from a six-month deployment in the Mediterranean Sea, March 11, 1948, to throngs of family and friends eager to see their sailors.

Members of the 43rd Infantry Division marched down Granby Street in parade formation November 11, 1951, before sailing the next day to join General Dwight D. Eisenhower's forces in Europe.

Four

A Navy Christmas

"Whose heart hath ne'er within him burned,
As home his footsteps he hath turned,
From wandering on a foreign strand?"

—From *Love of Country*, n.d.
Sir Walter Scott, English novelist and poet
(1771–1832)

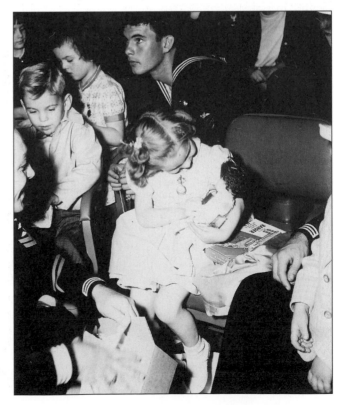

On October 29, 1953, Captain James H. Flatley, USN, sent a letter home to the families of personnel reporting for duty at Naval Air Station Norfolk, Virginia, which said, "The strength and efficiency of this air station in these critical times in world history depend in large measure upon the morale and spirit of the crew. You [the families] and I share the responsibility for keeping that morale and spirit at the highest point." Members of Fighter Squadron Twenty-One, redesignated Attack Squadron Forty-Three and, subsequently, VF-43 Challengers, enjoy a squadron Christmas party held December 21, 1957, on board Naval Air Station Oceana. (Photographer unknown.)

With the assistance of Navy volunteers, these little boys received new shoes for Christmas, c. 1943.

Staff at the USS Fairfax Residential Club at the Fairfax Hotel handed out gifts to sailors at a Christmas party in 1944. The club was home to servicemen who could not be provided living arrangements on military installations in Norfolk, hence the name, "residential club."

On the Danish ship *Gudron Maersk*, out of Copenhagen, Chief Steward Kanut Petersen decorated two trees in the saloon for the crew's Yule feast, December 24, 1950. The universality of the celebration of the birth of Christ was evident in Norfolk's harbor as crews of merchant ships from many lands observed Christmas traditions of their native countries. They thought of home, said prayers for peace, and talked through the night. As is the custom in Denmark before the dinner, crewmen placed one of their Christmas trees in the middle of the room, joined hands, and circled around the tree singing the "Christmas Song."

HARBOR
"'Waist-deep,' her laden vessels came,
With torn and storm-stained sails.
Driving through the drifting fog
By grace of nerves—and 'lead.'
Sea-racked, salt-ruined and shaken,
By the fury of the gales,
Battered, worn, and leaking,—
But the sky breaks blue o'erhead,
And the buoy that looms on the starboard bow,
Is the harbor buoy—red.
And so at this Merry Christmas-tide,
Deep-laden from the ports afar,
Safe from the storms and gales 'outside,'
From shifting shoal and treacherous bar,
May your ship, in harbor, safely ride,
And her 'riding-light' be the Christmas star."
—William C. Norman, 1929

Crewmen of the *Gudron Maersk* enjoyed a Christmas dinner featuring roasted goose, elaborate Danish side dishes, and an ample supply of wine, beer, and brandy for those who wanted it. Following dinner, they exchanged small gifts and prayed together. The goose was near perfection as the ship's cook checked his main course (top).

Three Italian cooks fussed over special Christmas cakes on the *Clella Campanella*. The Italian crew had a Christmas Eve dinner that included roasted lamb and chicken as the main course, and following the dinner, crewmen went ashore for midnight Mass. Captain Giovanti Bianciotto allowed each of his crew a short ration of brandy and one holiday meal on Christmas Day which included numerous Italian specialties.

Santa arrived by helicopter, ferried from the North Pole by Lieutenant Edward J. Larkin, USN. Santa Claus landed on the escort carrier USS *Mindoro*'s (CVE-120) flight deck on December 23, 1951, and was welcomed by swarms of children who were guests of the ship's crew. Santa, portrayed by Boatswain's Mate C.L. Jones, gathered the children about him on a forward elevator and they went below to the hangar bay for a party around a huge Christmas tree. The helicopter is an HO3S-1. (Jim Mays, photographer.)

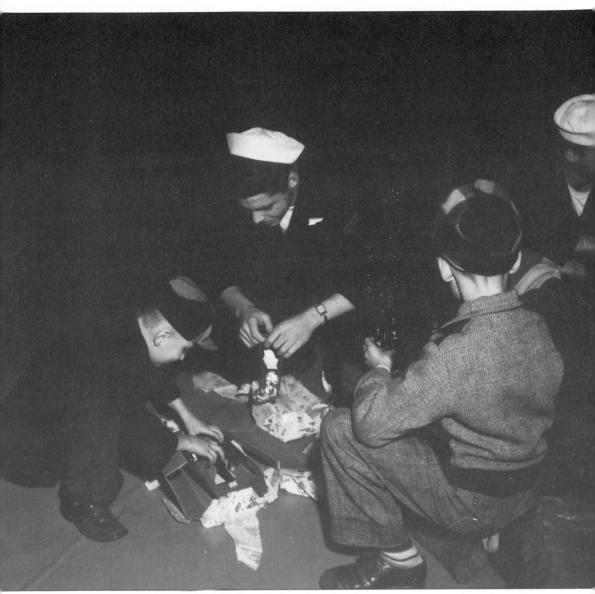

SANTA CLAUS KNOWS WHERE DADDY IS.

The whereabouts and movements of Navy ships may not always be known to the families of sailors, but Santa Claus knows where the ships are at all times. Up and down the East Coast, in Atlantic waters, Guantanamo Bay, Mediterranean Sea, and Persian Gulf, preparations are made for Christmas, dedicated to the Prince of Peace. Navy gray paint is the background for myriad holiday scenery, from brilliantly lighted Christmas trees and garlands to greetings and packages from home. In days gone by, Christmas Day was children's day in the fleet. If ships were in an American or foreign port under peacetime conditions, Santa Claus, arriving by seaplane, helicopter, or launch, made his way to the ships to entertain the children whom the sailors arranged to bring aboard for parties and presents. Unable to be with their own families, seeing children aboard ship on Christmas helped many sailors remember the joy of the holiday.

Crewmen of the aircraft carrier USS *Coral Sea* (CVB-43) had their Christmas party at Norfolk City Arena on both December 2 and 3, 1952, because there were simply too many sailors to fit all of them in the room for one night.

Enlisted crewmen of the destroyer tender USS *Everglades* (AD-24) entertained elderly women from the Mary F. Ballentine Home for the Aged and Lydia H. Roper Home for the Aged, December 23, 1953. Seventeen ladies between the ages of sixty-five and ninety-five were escorted by sailors they dubbed their "grandson escorts." Sailors treated their "grandmothers" to a turkey dinner with all the trimmings and presented them with wool stoles as Christmas presents. The oldest woman present was Stella Ferebee, whose uncle, Thomas R. Ballentine, provided the financing for the Ballentine Home in 1903. Ferebee was ninety-five years old. One of Ferebee's ninety-year-old contemporaries remembered sailing on the USS *Constitution*, "Old Ironsides," and the USS *Monitor*, the famous Union ironclad. Participating *Everglades* enlisted men paid for the dinner, including taxi fare for their guests, out of pocket. (Jim Mays, photographer.)

The aircraft carrier USS *Franklin D. Roosevelt* (CVA-42) returned from six-month deployment on December 2, 1953. "Hey Babe, It's Me!" was a happy reunion of sweethearts, while the two brothers (below) got reacquainted with their parents. (Jim Mays, photographer.)

Volunteers at the Navy YMCA assisted sailors with package wrapping, December 3, 1955. The Navy YMCA was a busy place, as thousands of sailors brought in their Christmas gifts to be done up in bright-colored tissue and cheerful outer wrappings and then mailed all over the country. Women from several civic organizations and individual volunteers took care of wrapping duties. (Jim Mays, photographer.)

Five
Christmas in the City

"I will honour Christmas in my heart and try to keep it all the year."

—From *A Christmas Carol*, 1843
Charles Dickens, English author (1812–1870)

There were only seventeen shopping days until Christmas, and the weather was clear and crisp as shoppers ventured into the shores along Granby Street on December 5, 1937, to do their gift buying early. Norfolk's retail district was crowded from morning to night. The stores, counters piled high with merchandise and extra sales clerks on hand, were doing a thriving business. Full effects of the general business recession nationwide were not felt in Norfolk, and most retailers of the period did not expect the city to be as seriously affected as more industrial centers of the United States.

Christmas.

With hearty Greetings and all good Wishes.

Christmas cards sent to and from people in Norfolk carried on the custom of sharing the holidays among friends and family initiated by Sir Henry Cole in England in 1843. The first card was designed by J.C. Horsley, and he had it commercially printed and sold in London. William Egley, another English artist, produced a popular Christmas greeting card in 1849. Themes on the cards reflect Christmas customs practiced around the world, including winter landscapes, animals, and cartoons. The Christmas card shown here was printed and sold in 1885 by Wirths Bros & Owen, a British company, from a scene drawn by Albert Bowers.

Marked only with the initials "St. J.T.," this Christmas card with the delicate and cherubic little girls who have come upon a bird's nest, harkens to the good luck symbolized when someone makes such a find in the Christmas tree. The card was made in the Victorian-era, c. 1880.

At this merry Christmas time Best wishes come to thee and thine.

With loving Christmas Greetings.

This little Christmas greeting was fashioned by Raphael Tuck & Sons, c. 1895, and it depicts the popular Victorian image of a small child with a favorite toy. Raphael Tuck & Sons was a British printing company which promoted itself as "the art publishers to their majesties the King and Queen."

SANTA CLAUS IS A NORFOLK BOOSTER

"Santa Claus is a Norfolk Booster" appeared in the *Virginian-Pilot* newspaper on December 15, 1913. Christmas retail sales and the city's overall economy were excellent at that time.

707 Baldwin Place

Heartiest Greetings for A Very Merry Christmas and Happy New Year

John A. Gurkin

John A. and Pearl B. Gurkin moved to 707 Baldwin Avenue in North Ghent sometime in 1920/21, and they sent this postcard to friends and business associates during Christmas 1921 to show them their new home. Gurkin was the owner of Gurkin Electric Company, an electrical contracting business, and mayor of Norfolk from September 1, 1938, to August 31, 1940. John A. Gurkin resided at his spacious Baldwin Avenue house until 1977.

A display window at Shulman's, located on the bottom floor of the Monticello Hotel, was filled with samples of the Girl Scouts' contributions to underprivileged children and an advertisement for public support of their Christmas cause, *c.* December 1930.

Salvation Army members stood at their designated posts outside popular establishments and on busy street corners throughout Norfolk every Christmas season, even during the Great Depression. This photograph was taken on December 4, 1933.
"And from the fulness of his heart he fished / A dime for Jesus who had died for men." [From *Karma*, 1925; Edwin Arlington Robinson, American poet (1869–1935).]

The Christmas rush was complicated by Norfolk's heaviest snowfall, deposited by a nor'easter on December 22, 1935, the day before this picture was taken. Snow remained piled high in all its splendor, clogging urban transportation facilities throughout the city. A City Hall Avenue traffic jam, looking toward Bank Street at the old City Hall building, kept shoppers and delivery men from reaching their appointed destinations in timely fashion.

The first Community Christmas Festival held in Norfolk was staged on the banks of the Hague, December 21, 1938. Hundreds of city residents went to hear choirs and glee clubs join a chorus of one thousand voices in singing Christmas carols and hymns. Planned on an elaborate scale, the Community Christmas Festival told the story of the nativity in its six tableaux.

Snow fell in time for Christmas, December 24, 1939.

CHRISTMAS EVE

Tonight the Christmas candles glow
Thru many a frosted window pane
Because from the star that long-ago
Shone brightly over Bethlehem's plain
"Peace, peace on earth," the angels sang
"All glory be to God on high"
And loud the vaults of Heaven rang
As myriad voices filled the sky
Oh! blest that night was Bethlehem
For Christ was born of Mary there;
And the star his royal diadem
Proclaimed his kingdom everywhere
For still we hear the Heavenly choir
That carolled at our Saviour's birth
Still see the star of Heavenly fire
That sheds his light o'er all the earth.
—William C. Norman, *c.* 1927

This is one of the many beautiful neighborhood nativity scenes in Norfolk, 1938. A popular folk belief was that the oxen kneel every Christmas just as the oxen kneeled in the manger the night of Christ's birth. "Christmas Eve, and twelve of the clock. / 'Now they are all on their knees,' / An elder said as we sat in a flock / By the embers in hearthside ease." [From *The Oxen*, 1916; Thomas Hardy, English poet (1840–1928).]

Lines such as the ones in this photograph, taken December 21, 1940, paraded unendingly before the parcel windows at Norfolk's main post office during the Christmas rush. Arms laden with Christmas packages, customers mailed in the largest number of parcels ever sent through the Norfolk post office at that time. Both incoming and outgoing regular mail was also the heaviest in the post office's history.

Picking out a Christmas tree at the City Market was a tradition in old Norfolk. This photograph, *c.* 1941, conjures the scent of evergreens and fresh cut flowers, smells which wafted through the air as throngs of people chattered away, selected a tree, perhaps some mistletoe and a wreath before loading up and going home.

Christmas window shopping brought smiles to great crowds of parents and their children who delighted in the laughing, mechanical Santa Claus in the window of W.G. Swartz Company on Granby Street. Christmas was two weeks away when this picture was taken on December 9, 1944. Yuletide greens and berries had yet to arrive in Norfolk and greenery such as youpon, holly, mistletoe, and pine boughs were not being sold on the local market. The lack of labor to cut Maine firs and scarcity of shipping space left dealers of local cedars and pines the sole purveyors of Christmas trees that year. Tree ornaments were virtually unavailable in 1944. From the happy faces, the spirit of Christmas was in abundant supply.

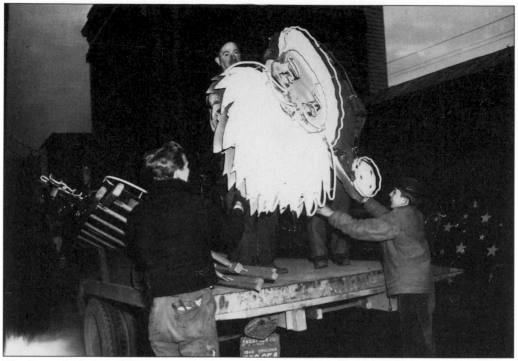

The beautiful lights of Christmas which graced downtown buildings for the holidays eventually had to be taken down and stored away for another year. Workers dismantled a large, lighted Santa Claus decoration on January 3, 1948, along the 400-block of Granby Street.

Norfolk residents purchased many beautiful wreaths and decorative Christmas greens at the City Market over the years. In this photograph, taken December 9, 1950, a young woman buys a wreath from one of the vendors. As Carroll H. Walker, famed Norfolk photographic historian, once recalled, "the minute you stopped to look at something, they'd come over to you and say 'What can I help you with?' Everything was different then. That was the center of Norfolk."

A Christmas flower vendor at the City Market checks her stock and arrangements, December 1948.

Twin dolls, dressed by Mrs. Thomas N. Spessard (right), an assistant chairman of the Community Toy Shop, were selected by a mother as Christmas presents for her six-year-old twin daughters, December 15, 1950. The Community Toy Shop was sponsored by the Norfolk Fire Division, the Council of Social Agencies, and radio station WTAR, and it opened at the Army Organized Reserve Headquarters at the corner of Duke Street and Brambleton Avenue the day before this picture was taken. (Jim Mays, photographer.)

Laurie G. Trego of Sharpley Circle smilingly displays the traditional mistletoe she purchased in downtown Norfolk on December 23, 1950, along with pine boughs, to decorate her home. (Jim Mays, photographer.)

Selling a customer on the finer points of tree has always been part of the holiday trade for vendors. This transaction took place December 24, 1950, at one of the innumerable tree lots which proliferated the city.

The chef at the Monticello Hotel prepares to cook a traditional Virginia New Year's Day sidedish of "hog jowls and black-eyed peas," December 31, 1950. The recipe which follows is the one most commonly used for this very Southern dish.

HOG JOWLS AND BLACK-EYED PEAS

1 cup dried black-eyed peas
3 cups water
3 small white onions, peeled but not sliced
1/4 pound hog jowl, cut into 1/2-inch cubes
1 teaspoon salt
1/4 teaspoon fresh ground pepper

Sift through the peas, culling out partial or split peas, and wash them. Place the peas in a medium Dutch oven. Cover with water 2 inches above peas and bring to a boil. Cook 5 minutes. Remove from heat; let peas stand 1 hour in covered pot. Drain well.

Place peas, 3 cups water, onions, hog jowl, salt and pepper in the Dutch oven. Bring to a boil. Reduce heat, cover and simmer another hour or until peas are tender. Makes enough for four servings.

The first Salvation Army booth to be opened at Wards Corner was sponsored by the Wards Corner Lions Club and manned by volunteers. Wilbert Will (left) hands the kettle to Lieutenant Polly Elder, as Tom Wasserman looks on, December 8, 1953. The Lions Club manned the booth for two of the days it was open, and various other civic organizations volunteered to man the location when the Salvation Army could not provide personnel support.

W.L. Pool (left), the Tanners Creek representative to the Board of Supervisors of Norfolk County, bought the first Christmas tree in the fourth annual Christmas tree sale sponsored by the Crossroads Lions Club from Lions President Clifton Downes, December 14, 1953. (Jim Mays, photographer.)

Wreath sellers came from Princess Anne County to sell their greenery in front of City Arena in 1958. Christmastime in Norfolk in days gone by had a character all its own. Sidewalk wreath makers weaved trailing cedar sprigs, holly, and pine cones into magnificent creations. (Orby G. Kelley Jr., photographer.)

The F.W. Woolworth's Department Store on Granby Street carried a "Make Your Own Ornaments" display which endured for many years. This photograph was taken by an unknown photographer in 1960.

This is a Christmas dinner at Norfolk Union Mission, 1958.

"I heard the bells on Christmas Day
  Their old familiar carols play,
  And wild and sweet
  The words repeat
  Of peace on earth, good will to men."

—From *Christmas Bells*, 1841
Henry Wadsworth Longfellow (1807–1882)

Six

Children's Smiles and Santa Visits

"The stockings were hung by the chimney with care,
In hopes that St. Nicholas soon would be there. . ."

—From *A Visit from St. Nicholas*, composed November 23, 1823
Clement Clarke Moore, American lexicographer and poet
(1779–1863)

Children hang their stockings on the mantle for Santa Claus, *c.* Christmas Eve, 1900.

Frances Adams and her doll, which appeared on Christmas morning 1905.

Invoices kept at the Library of Congress show that in March 1759, the estate of Daniel Parke Custis (the late husband of Martha, future wife of George Washington) had purchased toys which would have delighted any child. They came from a firm with the enchanting name of Unwin and Wrigglesworth, and included the following:

"A child's fiddle,
A coach and six in a box,
A stable with six horses,
A corner cupboard,
A neat walnut bureau,
A filigree watch,
A neat enameled watch box,
A toy whip,
A child's huzzit."

Frances Adams, pushing, is pictured here with Doris Kemp, c. 1905. Frances and her friend, Doris, lived next door to one another on Lincoln Street, located one block west of Church Street between Virginia Beach Boulevard and Brambleton Avenue. (Photographer unknown.)

Hundreds of children defied extremely cold weather to bring food and toys for less fortunate boys and girls and to see a children's show at Loew's State Theatre on Granby Street, December 21, 1935. The price of admission was an article of clothing, a toy, or some kind of non-perishable food. This photograph shows about half the contributions received that day by the Christmas Joy Fund, then in its second year.

FUND BRINGS JOY TO CHILDREN AT CHRISTMAS
The Christmas Joy Fund was begun by the *Virginian-Pilot* and the *Ledger-Dispatch* in 1934 to offset the suspension of direct federal relief for those in financial straits. Many children would have gone without a visit from Santa Claus and numerous adults without food for Christmas if the Norfolk newspapers had not inaugurated the Joy Fund. In its first year of operation, the Joy Fund raised nearly $6,000 to distribute toys to over two thousand children and provided holiday baskets for more than 1,200 families. After their first try at holiday fund-raising, the Norfolk newspapers elicited cooperation from a group of welfare agencies, and with their new partners, they have continued the tradition of the Joy Fund ever since. Symbolic of the kind of appeal by a parent received by the newspaper in 1935 was a letter from a mother who wrote, "I am a widow and have one son. He has no clothes, and I have no clothes, and I would like to have a basket, too. Anything be very highly esteem."

Not all children have been fortunate enough to have families at Christmas. The baby boy on the rocking rooster and the other small children in the photograph (top left) were residents of the DePaul Hospital children's ward, and many of them had varying degrees of polio, c. 1940. A nun who worked in the ward holds two of the babies (bottom right).

Photographer Charles S. Borjes went on assignment with staff writer Warner Twyford to photograph these children for a *Virginian-Pilot* cover story about the Kenny polio treatments at DePaul. Though initially wary of being in the same room as children with polio, Borjes was coaxed into the ward and through his camera lens, fell in love with the children.

Christmas morning 1940 brought out these three cowpokes, two of them totin' guns. Santa Claus outfitted little boys around Norfolk with cap guns, pop guns, rocket rifles, and, of course, the necessary holster sets, cowboy hats, and requisite cowpoke-wear resembling that worn by William S. Hart, Gene Autry, Roy Rogers, Hopalong Cassidy, and the Cisco Kid in all the movie books and picture shows.

A Christmas party was held at the Edgewater Home for Girls on December 20, 1948.

Santa arrived at the Center Shops on 21st Street on November 24, 1950, and was welcomed by throngs of young children. Old St. Nick worked hard to hear the wishes of Norfolk children until Christmas Eve when he departed on his rounds to deliver packages to children around the world.

Santa Claus visits have enthralled children in Norfolk for decades. This photograph, taken in 1950 by *Virginian-Pilot* photographer Charles S. Borjes of unnamed children with Santa, speaks to the magic and enchantment of the holidays brought by the jolly man himself. Santa makes the rounds in Norfolk, and even the rest of the world. And under the red suit with the black belt and black boots and the white trimmings—well, you are sure to see something a little different about him every time. This is because he has got a pinch of moon dust in his beard and he can be what he wants to be.

Santa came to all of Norfolk's department stores during the holiday season to see children and give some of them a spin in his sleigh, minus the reindeer, of course. He joggled this youngster on his knee as his face curled up like somebody's grandfather smiling. In 1950, when this photograph was taken at the Center Shops, Santa said most little boys wanted trucks, bicycles, pistols, and boats, while most little girls wanted dolls, washing machines, and such. If a child could not remember what they wanted, starstruck at the sight of Santa, Santa could magically make them remember.

This was the Christmas manger scene at Ocean View Elementary School, December 1950.

Staff at the Children's Hospital of the King's Daughters provided Christmas decorations and a party for hospitalized children on December 15, 1953.

Little cowpoke Billy Sykes continued to enjoy the gifts under his Christmas tree as this photograph was taken on December 29, 1950.

The Doll Repair Center of the Community Toy Shop, operated by the Norfolk Fire Department in conjunction with various civic organizations and volunteers, worked Christmas miracles on about two thousand dolls with missing arms, legs, and heads, giving each one new limbs and paint during the 1951 holiday season. The doll repair loft was located on Boush Street above Newton's Florist. The transformation of some of the dolls was remarkable, evident by this photograph taken November 24.

THE COMMUNITY TOY SHOP
Someone at one of Norfolk's fire stations started thinking about hard times, unemployment, and Christmas back in 1925, and about all the repercussions that difficult periods have on Christmas for children of those unable to provide for little ones during the holidays. The fireman probably had children of his own and thought of how joyful the holiday was to them. After talking the problem over with other firemen, they decided to ask the public to donate toys which were broken but could be repaired and made to look like new. The public responded. People from all over Norfolk brought toys to the fire station on Bute Street. Toys came from homes of the wealthy and from homes of those not-so-wealthy, but each found a place side-by-side such as doll carriages discarded by little girls who had grown too old to play with them or wagons with bent axles, chipped paint, and the like. Dolls that were broken and scratched sat next to those almost new. Norfolk firemen devoted many between-fire hours to make Christmas happier for underprivileged children. Throughout the year, they would collect discarded and out-grown toys, which were taken to fire stations for restoration. These were the toys used to stock the Community Toy Shop, a project begun in 1944 and sponsored by the Norfolk Fire Division, the Council of Social Agencies, and radio station WTAR.

Firemen work to repair toys in a makeshift toyshop, while a group of eager little boys espy the firemen's treasure trove of bicycles, tricycles, and scooters, both images *c*. 1950.

Underprivileged children of all ages packed the City Auditorium on December 18, 1948, f or a party with Santa Claus put on by the Salvation Army and the Advertising Club of Norfolk. The jolly old gentlemen handed out over four thousand presents during the morning program, which enamored the children, especially those who had the opportunity to be on stage with Santa.

This nativity scene was presented by the Girls' Club of Norfolk at the tree-lighting ceremony held on Wednesday, December 16, 1951, at City Park. Players are, from left to right: (front) JoAnn Willoughby (wiseman), Angela Green (shepherd), Gloria Herring (shepherd), Patsy Stancil (Mary), and Vivien Ange (wiseman); (standing in the background) Frances Griffin (angel), Linda Newman (Joseph), and Faye Ange (wiseman).

The Norfolk Recreation Bureau set up mailboxes in front of elementary schools around the city for children to drop their letters to Santa Claus in a "U.S. Mail" box. This photograph was taken in front of J.E.B. Stuart Elementary School in Colonial Place, 1956.

The Norfolk Police Department had collected a diverse assortment of toys for underprivileged children, evident in this 1962 photograph. (Photographer unknown.)

Marguerite Westman, two-and-a-half-year-old daughter of Mr. and Mrs. J.R. Westman of 517 Burleigh Avenue, was up late the night of November 23, 1951, to greet the 27 1/2-foot figure of Santa Claus at Wards Corner. The post office building is in the background.

Seven

By River and Sea

"The snow lies sprinkled on the beach,
And whitens all the marshy lea:
The sad gulls wail adown the gale,
The day is dark and black the sea."

—From *The Snow Lies Sprinkled on the Beach*, 1890
Robert Bridges, English poet (1844–1930)

The Elizabeth River was frozen over completely when this photograph was taken on January 5, 1918. Merchant seamen crossed the waterway from ship to ship with ease. During the first week of January, waterborne traffic in the tributaries, rivers, and the Chesapeake Bay was at a standstill with the exception of the ferries and some tugs which plodded slowly across Norfolk waters. Seagoing vessels had suspended operations. At Virginia Beach and Cape Henry, the bay and the Atlantic Ocean were nothing but a broad expanse of ice as far as the eye could see.

Virginia Beach dunes were covered in snow and ice during a fierce winter storm in 1906. (Harry C. Mann, photographer.)

Virginia Beach dunes, covered in snow, blend into this wooded area, Fort Story, *c.* 1906. (Harry C. Mann, photographer.)

This image shows the Lafayette River near the Hampton Boulevard Bridge, December 2, 1935.

Tanners Creek was frozen over between Colley Avenue and Hampton Boulevard on December 24, 1935, holding small boats in its icy grip.

A spectacular fire gutted the east half of the Norfolk County ferry terminal at the foot of Commercial Place on December 26, 1935. Ferry service between Norfolk and Portsmouth was halted for hours as firemen fought the two-alarm blaze in frigid weather. Seven firemen were injured as they fought the blaze which had, at first, threatened to raze the pine-and-stucco structure. Northwest winds, razor-sharp with subfreezing temperatures, made the firefighting a bitter and dangerous job. Rapid emergency operations by ferry officials resulted in resumption of pedestrian ferry traffic by evening in the west slip, while fire smoldered in the other two slips. Vehicular traffic was restored later in the evening. The ferry terminals were rebuilt soon after the fire.

Winter weather blasted Norfolk, leaving in its wake these pleasure boats stranded in an arm of the Lafayette River. The perspective is looking toward Morningside. The ice extended from bank to bank of the river on January 28, 1936. Northwest winds, blowing as high as 25 miles per hour in Norfolk, helped keep the temperature at 16 degrees. The mean temperature was only 20 degrees. This was 21 degrees below normal for the date and the coldest January 28 on records of the Norfolk Weather Bureau at that time. The large white boat on the left is the *Corelli. S.*

A fleet of fishing trawlers sought haven at the pier of the Boush Cold Storage plant at the foot of City Hall Avenue as Norfolk's harbor and Hampton Roads turned to veritable ice fields on the incoming tide on January 31, 1936. Huge blocks of ice were brought in by the tide from the James River and from points near Cape Henry. Near Cape Henry, there was an ice barrier several feet thick which encircled the beach line. As the tide came in, it wretched this ice barrier from the beach and swept it into Hampton Roads and the Elizabeth River.

The tug *J. Alvan Clark* plowed through the Elizabeth River on February 1, 1936.

A yacht was frozen in the Hague along Mowbray Arch and the terminus of Pembroke Avenue, February 2, 1936. Youngsters seized the opportunity to play in and around it.

Packed ice of varying thickness is shown at the Lesner Bridge, which crossed Lynnhaven Inlet, February 8, 1936.

Cottage Line residents at Ocean View hiked around on the ice which stretched as far out as the eye could see in front of their houses on February 8, 1936. Most of the ice floated down from upper Chesapeake Beach, and, with the temperature dropping, fresh ice welded the blocks together.

These boats take refuge at the piers adjacent to E.R. Clark & Company, located at the foot of Botetourt Street in Norfolk's Atlantic City section during the fierce snowstorms of February 1937.

This photograph was taken of the Chesapeake Bay from the shore off Ocean View Avenue on the Cottage Line at Ocean View, Saturday, February 8, 1939, looking northward up the bay. For several miles out to the main channel, the water was covered with ice. The people out on the ice to the left (standing together) were Frank S. Pace and his two children, Frank Jr. and Betty. The whiteness of the ice and the contrasting dark, cloudless sky led Norfolk residents to believe beyond the horizon lay the North Pole, but despite the looks of it, the Arctic was just as far away as ever.

The jetty was completely frozen over, and ice flows in the Atlantic created serious hazards throughout the Chesapeake Bay, on January 29, 1940. While there was considerable ice in the inner harbor, ice jams blocked some points in the bay. The United States Coast Guard cutter *McLane* reported that an unsuccessful attempt was made to break a channel from Crisfield to Horse Hammock and Smith Island. Smith Island residents were cut off from their source of food and medical attention. The *McLane* was bringing them provisions.

The refreshment stand at Ocean View had few takers for hot dogs and Orange Crush on January 29, 1940. Ocean View was wearing a bathing suit designed by Jack Frost and no one wanted to play.

Boats of the fishing fleet were encrusted in snow and ice after a storm during the winter of 1950. The location of these vessels was the Boush Cold Storage piers.

Eight
Winter Snow

When men were all asleep the snow came flying,
In large white flakes falling on the city brown,
Stealthily and perpetually settling and loosely lying,
Hushing the latest traffic of the drowsy town . . .

—From *London Snow*, 1880
Robert Bridges, English poet (1844–1930)

The snow of March 2, 1927, was recorded as one of the most significant in Norfolk's history, dropping 11 inches, as this picture of York Street shows. The snowstorm was accompanied by a shrieking nor'easter that brought down telephone and telegraph poles by the dozens and paralyzed rail and highway traffic. People were stranded in offices, unable to travel home by impassable roads. Schools closed just after lunch, followed by businesses. Snowdrifts were anywhere from 6 to 10 feet high. (H.D. Vollmer, photographer.)

This snowy scene shows Main Street and Market Square (Commercial Place). The photograph was taken in 1888 by E.L. Boyce. Boyce's photography studio was located at 176 Main Street near Talbot Street. The horse in the foreground stands where the Confederate Monument is today. The old market house can be seen to the upper left of the photograph. The market stalls in the foreground are where citizens of old Norfolk bought their Christmas dinners. Most of the marketplace site is now occupied by the twenty-three-story NationsBank building.

The winter of 1917/18 was bitterly cold. Freezing temperatures and frozen waterways were the norm. On December 31, 1917, temperatures reached a high of 16 degrees and a low of 9 degrees. The Elizabeth River filled with heavy ice, and its eastern and southern branches were frozen solid as was much of the James River. Dauntless Norfolk citizens devised creative modes of transportation. This mulemobile, pictured on Main Street near the Confederate Monument on January 3, 1918, was surely one of those. Another blizzard hit on January 5, making conditions even worse. (Photographer unknown.)

The No. 5 engine headed down East Main Street between Addington Lane and Talbot Street toward a minor fire, January 4, 1918. After the fire of January 1, which destroyed four buildings, nothing to follow could be worse. (Photographer unknown.)

Heavy snow and ice stopped streetcars on their tracks throughout the city as shown in this image taken January 3, 1918, on East Main Street. The Gladstone Hotel is indicated by the "X" over the building in the center of the picture. (Photographer unknown.)

The snowstorm of February 27, 1924, created blizzard-like conditions for pedestrians who struggled throughout the day along downtown streets.

Norfolk was experiencing its heaviest snowfall in seven years when an enterprising young man built his snow*woman* on February 24, 1934. Guess who the lady is? Clue: She was internationally known as a singer of "hot" numbers in the late 1920s and 1930s and starred in such Paramount films as *Night After Night, She Done Him Wrong,* and *I'm No Angel.* As she once said, "You may admire a girl's curves on first introduction, but the second meeting shows up new angles." If you still haven't guessed, turn to the bottom of page 128 for the answer!

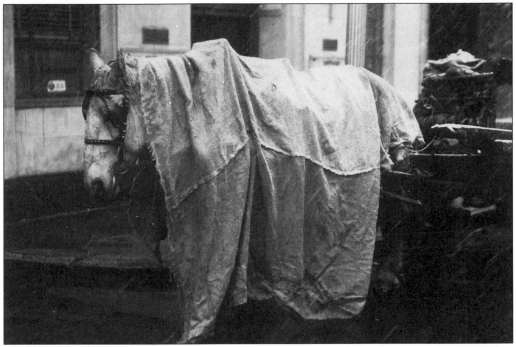

A great snowstorm hit the city on March 10, 1934, but its huge flakes disappeared as fast as they struck the ground, and as a result, by nightfall, there was little evidence of the snow except on lawns and fields. Six to eight inches would have covered the ground had it not melted. Answering duty's call was this horse, pulling a delivery wagon, and a traffic officer at the intersection of Granby Street and City Hall Avenue.

The weather was clear and cold, the ice firm and slick. This invigorating combination enticed young and old to the lake at the new Lakeside Park in South Norfolk on January 31, 1935. Only a few of the people in the picture are wearing ice skates. Those without skates used either sleds or had fun skidding along the icy surface on their shoes. Crowds of hundreds of people had been on the pond for several days and nights. Relief from the cold spell which had gripped Norfolk for over a week finally came the day after this picture was taken as temperatures rose above freezing.

Skaters at Lakeside Park, South Norfolk, Wednesday, January 28, 1936, take advantage of perfect ice left by "King Winter" as temperatures in the city and surrounding areas averaged only 20 degrees. Ice skating reigned as the city's major outdoor sport.

"We knew, if 'twere colder; the water would freeze, / And then, all delighted, our skates we would seize; / We'd leave our math'matics and grammar behind, / And haste to the first icy lake we could find . . . " [From *The Skating Frolic—A Fact*, 1840; John Thomas Watson, American poet (1822–1905).]

Virginia Electric and Power Company linesmen climbed a power pole located at Gosnold and Delaware avenues in Colonial Place on Christmas Eve, 1935, to restore service. The city was experiencing its first white Christmas in more than ten years.

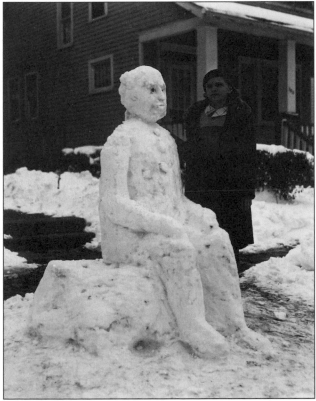

Vera Ackiss stands by General George Washington, done in snow by her father, O.L. Ackiss, of 206 West 29th Street, December 25, 1935. This icy work of art was completed during the heavy snowstorm which blanketed the city and provided endless entertainment for children of all ages.

Though not exactly a safe form of entertainment, this young man's trip down Boush Street behind an automobile on December 29, 1935, seems to have been enjoyable despite the risk to life and limb. Norfolk was in the grip of a major snow and ice storm which lasted at least two weeks. Ice conditions on the Chesapeake Bay were so bad that the United States Coast Guard cutter *Apache* had been breaking ice and rendering assistance to small boats caught in the bay and its tributaries for over a week when this picture was taken at the end of December.

While adults may have grumbled about the snow and ice, these youngsters took advantage of the inclement conditions to stage a snowball fight and build snowmen, December 30, 1935. The location of the photograph appears to be Pembroke Avenue in Ghent.

Johnny Boy and friends were caught by the camera on December 31, 1935.

A man stood up to his knees in snow at the corner of Main and Atlantic Streets, February 7, 1936, during a blizzard which dropped 9 inches of snow on the city. This was the third major storm of the 1935/36 winter, bringing the seasonal accumulation to 33.5 inches—an all-time record for the months of December, January, and February in Norfolk. This figure dated back to the establishment of the weather bureau in the city in 1871. The heaviest previous winter snowfall up to that time occurred in 1892/93, and it was 32.3 inches. The latter was accompanied by a note that that snowfall was the heaviest since the memorable winter of 1857. December of 1892 set the all-time record for single-month snowfall at 18.6 inches.

Young Frank Gregory was photographed in the snow-and-ice igloo he built on February 8, 1936, in front of his home at 220 Graydon Avenue. Norfolk was expecting another snowstorm to hit the next day. Norfolk residents had a name for their winter experiences, "the Ice Age of 1936," due to the severity of February's storms.

Streetcars came off their tracks at Monticello Avenue and Charlotte Street, derailed by the snow, February 7, 1936. Streetcar service was suspended as an icy wind whipped through Norfolk streets and brought the city to a standstill.

The snow had fallen throughout the night before, leaving the two girls depicted here a winter wonderland in which to play along the Hague. H.D. Vollmer shot this enchanting scene from Fairfax Avenue looking across to Mowbray Arch in historic Ghent, February 9, 1936.

Children fortunate enough to have sleds used the steps and area in front of Ohef Sholom Temple on Stockley Gardens for sledding on February 28, 1937. The snow, about 6 inches in all, was light and fleecy—perfect for snowballing and sledding. Nearly every child in the city was out playing in the snow, and they were joined by hundreds of adults who enjoyed snowballing and sled rides as much as the youngsters.

Many car owners had their work cut out for them to clear their vehicles of snow and ice. This lovely view of Fairfax Avenue looking west across the Hague in Ghent, February 28, 1937, shows the handiwork of one of the city's ten new snowplows at that time. Snowplows were rigged and ready to clear principal streets. This was the first time city officials had planned and executed a snow clearance plan in conjunction with Virginia Electric and Power Company. Previous snowstorms paralyzed the city, but thorough preparation and purchase of snow clearance equipment made the difference. Traffic was never seriously affected and streetcars, buses, and cars were able to move freely on nearly all streets in the city.

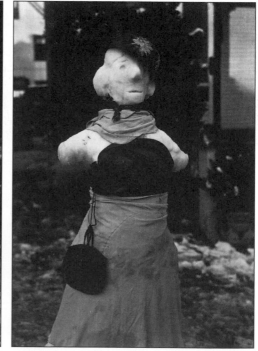

Snowmen popped up all over the city after the 9-inch snowfall of January 16, 1939. The distinguished snowman shown here is half the celebrity pair fashioned by Nancy Williamson and Frank Kellam. This is the Clark Gable of snowmen. His female companion was another Mae West knockout. Nice couple, eh?

As the war in Europe raged, subtle signs that its personalities had permeated our popular culture were beginning to appear, perhaps grotesquely at times. An Adolf Hitler snowman was conceived by Bill Ames and David Easter at Colley Avenue and Thirty-Fifth Street, hardly typical of the whimsical and happy figures normally seen on Norfolk street corners. The figures in the above picture depict a snowman couple out walking their dog at 1100 Graydon Avenue, January 9, 1940.

Creeks and coves in Norfolk were coated with ice, while temperatures in the city dropped as low as 15 degrees and never rose higher than 31 degrees on February 9, 1947. Winds from the west and northwest produced bitter cold conditions for pedestrians, but made for beautiful scenes such as this one in Lakeside Park, South Norfolk.

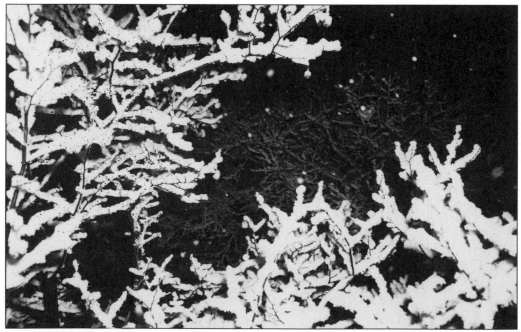

Heavy snow came down in the trees on Stockley Gardens, February 22, 1947. Most of Virginia was paralyzed by the late-February snowfall which measured anywhere from a depth of 27 inches in Dickenson County, the greatest in the state, to lesser levels around Roanoke, Lynchburg, Richmond, and Norfolk.
"The snow had begun in the gloaming, / And busily all the night / Had been heaping field and highway / With a silence deep and white." [From *The First Snowfall*, 1849; James Russell Lowell, American poet (1819–1891).]

Norfolkians scrambled for coal at Superior Coal Company, located at 1563 East Princess Anne Road, January 31, 1948, as bitter cold temperatures and heavy snow began to fall on the city.

Three young girls are ready to toss their snowballs at friends in Stockley Gardens, February 3, 1951. Numbing cold as low as 18 degrees greeted early-morning risers throughout the city. While motorists slipped and slid in a winter wonderland, youngsters took advantage of the snow to have snowball fights, build snowmen, and go sledding. The snow accumulated about 3 inches, making it the deepest snow locally since the 9.7-inch fall of February 9–10, 1948.

Nine

Will Spring Ever Come?

"Nothing is so beautiful as spring . . ."

—From *Spring*, 1918
Gerard Manley Hopkins, English poet
(1844–1889)

These three little darlings were on their way to Easter Sunday services at First Presbyterian Church of Norfolk, located at the corner of Colonial and Redgate avenues, April 13, 1941. Spring fashions had changed, even for the little ladies, in 1941. Sunday's Easter parade featured smartly tailored suits in purple, golden beige, spring blue, chartreuse, pink, and orchid. Soft plaids, new navies, and distinctive blacks gave variety to ladies' and girls' Easter attire.

Two little girls smile broadly and display their Easter bunny baskets, April 21, 1930. Perfect springlike weather and sunny skies drew church-goers from city streets to Ocean View and Virginia Beach for Easter parades by the sea. The number of promenaders at Ocean View during the afternoon was estimated at six thousand, while conservative estimates placed the number around twenty thousand at Virginia Beach.

Photographer Charles S. Borjes originally called this photograph, *Shark Riding*, but William N. Cox, sports editor of the *Virginian-Pilot* (seated in front), and friend were really "riding" a porpoise, first cousin of the dolphin. Porpoises are common along the coasts of the North Atlantic from Davis Strait down to New Jersey, where their chief food source consists of mackerel, herring, sole, whiting, and several varieties of crustaceans. Though porpoises are coast lovers, it is unclear how the one pictured here ended up in Norfolk. Porpoises frequently become entangled in fishermen's nets and drown because they cannot get to the surface. The picture was taken March 2, 1931.

The first commercial enterprise permitted in a United States Post Office building was set up in the Norfolk Federal Building by a blind man named Henderson T. Hedrick Jr. who asked President Franklin D. Roosevelt for the privilege. No rent was charged Hedrick, shown here behind the counter of his newsstand operation on February 7, 1935, three days after opening for business.

The gala opening of William S. Wilder's Colley Theatre, located in the 1500 block of Colley Avenue, on February 24, 1936, was a lavish affair attended by the leading citizens of Norfolk and Portsmouth who watched the first Norfolk showing of the Warner Brothers picture *Midsummer Night's Dream*. WTAR broadcast a radio program from the sidewalk in front of the theatre. Wilder was in attendance at the opening of the Colley Theatre, the sixth Wilder theatre in Virginia.

This happy threesome donned rollerskates and took to the streets of Ghent on April 6, 1938. They were Helen Warren, Mrs. John Maddrey, and Rebekah Huber.

These were just two of the thousands of men in uniform who attended Easter Sunday services in Ghent churches, April 5, 1942. The United States Marines in this photograph were arm-in-arm with girlfriends. Uniforms were seen throughout the churches of Norfolk as soldiers, sailors, and marines escorted wives, sweethearts, and girlfriends to church and socials.

Kite competitions take preparation. The youngsters in this picture were photographed at Larchmont Elementary School, March 16, 1943, getting their kites ready for the big contest four days later at City Park. In the picture are Earl Smith, Tom McCrory, Bobby Edmunds, Fraulein Ward, Billy Kohen, Billy Whitehurst, Vincent Ferebee, Jack Swan, Virginia Willis, Arthur Diamonstein, and Anne Horney.

These happy harbingers of spring were competitors in the first kite contest sponsored by the Norfolk Recreation Bureau on March 20, 1943, at City Park. Contestants, all boys fourteen years or younger, came out with their homemade creations, many of which sported World War II Army and Navy airplanes. They were joined by spectators, including old-time kite flyers who told youngsters about the art of making and flying kites. One of the old-timers flew his first kite in 1903.

Two Estonian little girls, Aimi Kuun (standing), age ten, and her seven-year-old sister, Inga (seated, far right), were attending Robert E. Lee School when this picture was taken on April 26, 1946. They had crossed the Atlantic in the fall of 1945 on a 37-foot sailboat with their parents, Captain and Mrs. Arvid Kuun, and twelve other Estonians on a 129-day voyage from Stockholm, Sweden. The Estonians fled their Baltic-state homeland because of Soviet occupation and oppression. Their little sailboat arrived off Cape Henry on December 14. The other two girls in the photograph with Aimi and Inga Kuun were (left to right) Ruth Gregory and Virginia Abbitt. The youngster to the extreme far left is unidentified.

Ann Louise, Barbara, and Christine Sawyer (left to right), triplet daughters of Mr. and Mrs. William W. Sawyer of 3004 Perrone Avenue, Fairmount Park, were celebrating their fifth birthday on February 8, 1950, when this photograph was taken. The triplets' mother celebrated her own birthday with Ann Louise, Barbara, and Christine, but was content to watch from the sidelines as her little girls rolled precariously about on their new roller skates. The Sawyers had six children, all of whom eventually attended Ballentine School. The triplets were thrilled with the potentialities of the bright steel skates. Tumbling about in the sun, their blonde curls bounced, and their blue eyes sparkled.

Some children and a dog were photographed playing in Broad Creek Village in 1950. (Jim Mays, photographer.)

Six-month-old triplets (left to right) Adair, Blair, and Clair, daughters of Mr. and Mrs. William Louis Archibald of Mears Corner in Princess Anne County (now part of Virginia Beach), were born on Halloween night 1950 at DePaul Hospital. The Archibalds owned a farm, and not to be outdone, one of their two milch goats gave birth to triplet billy kids on April 3, 1951. The other nannie goat had two little nannie kids and one billy kid four days later, making a total of two sets of kids triplets. Three sets of triplets on one farm was news, but it was also the first time anyone in the area had seen or heard of triplet goats. The photograph was taken on April 10, 1951. Flanking Adair, Blair, and Clair are their kid companions. The Archibald's oldest child, Billy (four-and-a-half years old), is holding one of the kids. Pauline, the couple's twenty-month old, is not shown.

Little Bobby Vincent and Fluffy relaxed while waiting for the pet show judges at the Boys' Club on the corner of 26th Street and Colonial Avenue, April 7, 1951. There were about 150 pet entries in the competition and most of them were puppy dogs. To the little fellows who entered them, the pedigree, or lack thereof, of their pup had little to do with the affectionate attachment between boy and dog. There were no losers in the competition since each boy won a prize.

Note: The answer to the question on the bottom of page 108 is Mae West.